Final Days. . .and Counting

Containing Instructions for Those Who Miss His Coming

Final Days...and Counting

Containing Instructions for Those Who Miss His Coming

by
Roy H. Hicks, D.D.

Unless otherwise indicated, all Scripture quotations are taken from the *King James Version* of the Bible.

Final Days. . .and Counting
Containing Instructions for Those Who Miss His Coming
ISBN 0-88144-155-4

Box 4113
San Marcos, CA 92069

Printed in the United States of America.

Contents

Introduction

The motivation for this book was a persistent, inward urge to begin to warn Christians about the words of our Lord Jesus, and the many other references in God's Word, about being ready for His coming. My burden is for the millions of people around the world who consider themselves to be Christians, but who may not in reality be ready for this great event.

Jesus taught that not everyone who says, "Lord, Lord," will enter into His Kingdom. (Matt. 7:21.) It's not enough just to be a believer in Christ, because even the devils believe. (James 2:19.)

Heaven is for the ones who do believe that Jesus is the Son of God, but who also have made Him the Lord of their lives. (Rom. 10:9,10.) Paul taught the necessity of being "found in him." (Phil. 3:9.) I had never really noticed how many people will be martyred by the anti-Christ for their refusal to bow down and worship Satan and take his number. They will die for their faith in Jesus. (Please note last chapter.)

My motivation for the first part of this book is two-fold: 1) to warn Christians to be ready for the coming of our Lord, and 2) to leave some instructions about a course to take for the millions of people who will be left behind.

The final part of this book is dedicated to a subject about which there is much confusion. There is far too much perplexity concerning the Lord's coming. There is the position of pre-tribulation, post-tribulation, and mid-tribulation; rapture, no rapture; millennium, no millennium! So much so that millions of Christians not only are confused but are almost totally ignorant of the subject.

I am continually surprised at the number of people, both in the Church and in the world, who have no knowledge of the European Common Market and of how fast things are moving toward the end.

Please read this book carefully. It will help you if you are ready, and will be a means of rescue if you are not. There is a way to heaven if one misses the coming of the Lord Jesus.

It would have been a lamentable thing to have lived in the days of our Lord's first coming, to have heard rumors of His ministry and of His death on the cross. . .and yet to have missed it by being so busy with just the mundane affairs of life. It is equally unthinkable to be alive in the time of His return. . .and miss it.

There are abundant signs of the times everywhere. Read them, hear them, and be ready. Be looking for, and loving, His appearance. (2 Tim. 4:8.)

1
Seven Letters

> **Blessed is he that readeth, and they that hear the words of this prophecy, and keep those things which are written therein: for the time is at hand.**
>
> **Revelation 1:3**

No credible book written on eschatology (the end-times) can ignore the seven letters to the seven churches under the authority of the Apostle John. The revelation of Jesus Christ (Head of the Church) to John is not a new one inasmuch as John had already seen and been with Jesus for many years. An important word from Jesus to John was that He is the Christ of the past, present, and future! (vv. 4,8,11,17,18.)

The reader of the book of Revelation, especially the first three chapters, must acknowledge that this book is part of God's Word to us and is not to be discarded because of the degree of difficulty in understanding and relating it to the future.

If pastors and writers fail to warn of the imminence of Christ's return, then an eternal, tragic disservice will have been rendered to multitudes of sincere people who simply have become caught up in the daily round of temporal activities.

Reader, if nothing else, this book is meant to disturb you. . .to shock you into examining your life. If you need to repent of sins, either of commission or omission, then I urge you to do so now!

The author has not allowed for an in-depth treatment of all seven of the churches written about in the book of Revelation. Many scholars believe that the first five churches (each representing a different period of time) have already become history. If so, it is important to the subject of eschatology that we address the sixth and seventh letters, especially since we are now in that time period in Church history.

In each period of time, the Lord Jesus has always admonished the churches to be overcomers. This is especially important in these last days. If there are saints in heaven, they must arrive there as a result of living an overcoming Christian life, or as a result of a "death bed" experience of receiving Jesus as personal Savior and Lord.

It is clearly taught throughout the Bible that a "one-time" confession of Jesus as Savior is not enough to assure eternal salvation. It takes a constant, daily, overcoming lifestyle. There will be no backslidden believers in heaven! All must repent, confess, and overcome! Faith must be proven by actions! (James 1:18 TCNT.)

The sixth church, the church in Philadelphia, seems to be the ideal church. It is the one which identifies with our present-day Church that is to be raptured. This church has great qualities: good works, an open door, and strength the other churches lacked.

This church will have had a greater influence on the Jews than any other church in history. Today many Jews identify with us Christians. They have received Jesus as their Messiah and worship at His feet, as we do. By the latest estimate, there are at least 50,000 Jewish believers.

Please note that this sixth church (representing our period in Church history) will be kept from the tribulation brought by the anti-Christ. This event had not yet come to pass when John wrote this prophecy, but lay in the future. This church, because it is a worshipping people who love God's Word and who engage in continuous fellowship with Him, is to be exempt from the tribulation, that period of worldwide suffering and wrath brought on by the cruel reign of the beast. (Rev. 14.) They will be kept from this hour of testing and also from God's wrath.

The above description fits a church organization of Holy Spirit-minded believers, of which there are now thousands and tens of thousands. *Please notice that this is the only one of the seven churches Jesus has promised to come and rescue.* And He will come, not only to keep them from that terrible hour that is coming upon the earth, but also to give them great reward for their faithfulness.

This raptured, "snatched," "caught-up" host of people, symbolized by the church in Philadelphia, will become a part of that great city, New Jerusalem. A born-again Christian — one who worships God daily and who has a hunger for His Word, one who has prayed for and done all he can to witness to Israel to turn to their true Messiah — will be a partaker of that great and wonderful event!

Such a believer as described above is almost an oddity in today's church world. Jude referred to the last days, calling attention to the mockers: those who do not seem to honor the Holy Spirit and do not pray in, or with, the Holy Spirit. (Jude 18-20.) In failing to do so, they have not built themselves up, and so will be torn down.

This "caught-up" church (worshipping believers) will receive the special reward of being a part of the temple of God, never to depart from it. According to Revelation 3:10-12, written upon them will be the name of God, the name of the city of God, and, finally, the new name of Jesus. Hallelujah!

Why would God so greatly honor this limited few (in comparison to the millions of saints in past history)?

These are the ones who are ready, looking for, waiting upon, and expecting His coming. *It is the only group of saints of all the ages who will have no need, or time, to repent and make things right with their fellow man and with God.* (This subject is dealt with further in another chapter.)

The last church is the surviving Laodicean church, the one that is left alone after the rapture to face the wrath of the anti-Christ. Not much can be said for a church that once knew the Lord — and was counted to be His — but became worldly and wealthy and felt they had no needs.

Here in the third chapter of Revelation, Jesus addressed a letter to them. They must have been saved at one time. If not, Jesus would not have called them one of His churches. Neither would He have assigned an angel to them. But He did both of these things.

There is a profusion of the Laodicean spirit in all churches. People influenced by this spirit of Laodicea sit in church, looking pious, sneaking quick glances at their watches, attending services only if it is convenient. They offer token attendance, token gifts, token commitment. Sadly, about the only aspect of their Christianity that is not token is their critical and fault-finding spirit.

Our Lord Jesus implied, by using the term "lukewarm," that such people are neither Christian nor heathen, neither for nor against. To be cold to His embrace, but hot to the world and its pleasures and profits, is to be lukewarm.

After the Lord's strong rebuke and plea for these people to turn and repent, we see a profound picture of sadness in His face as He says to them: **Behold, I stand at the door, and knock: if any man hear my voice, and open the door, I will come in to him, and will sup with him, and he with me** (Rev. 3:20). Jesus is not far off. He knocks at the heart's door...but the latch is on the inside and no one can open the door except the one to whom He is calling.

We can believe the Bible! It says that there will be Christians so cold in their backslidden condition, so involved with the cares of this world, that they will be rejected and spewed out of the mouth of God.

Dear reader, if you have become a Laodicean Christian, wherever you may be, please heed Christ's warning. Repent and overcome temptation. Jesus did not accuse the Laodicean Christians of being adulterous, promiscuous, robbers, murderers, wife beaters, or child molesters! Just of being lukewarm. If He were to couch it in today's terminology, He might say to them, "Get in, or get out."

If you are out, you know it. If you are in, you know it. If you are only half-way, you are neither in nor out. Like the Laodiceans, you are "wretched, and miserable, and poor, and blind, and naked," but just don't know it.

There is still time to repent. Turn and go all out for the Lord! Remember, a journey of a thousand miles begins with just one step.

2
"If" — the Biggest Little Word

The Apostle Paul made very clear to the Thessalonian church the great truth of the coming resurrection of their loved ones, followed by the rapture. In his letter to the Corinthian church, he made clear another great truth that is so pertinent to us who are living in the very hour that this could take place!

Paul describes how fast the dead bodies will be changed, and how fast the living will leave this earth. He taught that this will transpire, **In a moment, in the twinkling of an eye. . .** (1 Cor. 15:52).

The Greek word translated "moment" here is *atomos,* which means "an 'atom' of time." This is the only place in Scripture that the word "atom" is found. Literalized, we will be changed, caught up with the dead saints, in an atomic second. This figures out to be faster than even the speed of light.

There will be no time to repent.

No time to say, "I'm sorry."

No time to confess wrongdoing.

Not a moment to pray.

This is not a book on theology. It is not an argument for Arminianism or against Calvinism. It is a book written to sound an alarm! We who live in the end time will have to be ready twenty-four hours a day! Saints who have gone before us had time, before impending death, to make things right with God and their fellow men. Jesus never warned believers to be ready to die. He did warn them to be ready for His coming.

The thief on the cross had time to call on the Lord Jesus. Even in the split moments before a fatal auto collision, there is time to say, "Jesus, help me!" We must be found "in Christ," in fellowship and harmony with God.

Some writers give a false hope that if you received Jesus as your Savior twenty years ago, you have no fear of being left behind at the time of the rapture. They say that grace was then imparted and you are forever safe from falling.

The Bible contains the word "if" hundreds of times. These "ifs" are not God's responsibility. They belong to us — the believers. Dr. McBirney, a well-known radio preacher and teacher, made a great statement. He said, "It isn't enough to believe in Jesus. *You must make Him Lord of your life.*"

A very familiar statement has been around for years: "If He is not Lord of all, He is not Lord at all." All seem to agree that Romans 10:9 should read, ". . .confess with thy mouth, 'Jesus is Lord.'" We can all understand the word "Lord." Jesus must be Lord, King, Ruler, Master, Teacher, Leader. . .and even Dictator of our lives.

This great word "if" must have full meaning. If Jesus is accepted as Lord, then one can believe that God raised Him from the dead and that salvation has come to his soul.

Because of the great number of times the word "if" is used in the Bible, we are limited to only noting a few. In Colossians 1:23 the Apostle Paul uses an "if" in his great presentation of our Lord Jesus, the cross, the blood, and the reconciliation. He states, ***If* ye continue in the faith grounded and settled. . . .** J.B. Phillips' translation of this verse states it well, **This reconciliation assumes, of course, that you maintain a firm position in the faith.** This is not an author's opinion. This is the Word of God.

We are not dealing with legalism. Legalism is identified as the outward rules of dress, how we spend our leisure time, etc., and is not being addressed here.

There is no eternal reconciliation if one does not continue in his or her confession of faith. Paul, writing to Timothy, uses this expression again in 1 Timothy 2:15. *The Amplified Bible* states it thusly: **...they will be saved [eternally] if they continue in faith and love and holiness, with self-control....**

God's promises are conditional. Man does not surrender his will even when he receives Jesus as Lord. Man's will is eternal. Even in heaven he will have a will...but not willfulness! If a man surrendered his will at salvation, he would no longer be as a man, but as an animal who has no will to choose heaven or hell.

John, the beloved disciple and writer, puts an "if" in a very clearly taught doctrine in his first chapter. He was not writing to sinners, but to saints: **...*if* we walk in the light, as he is in the light...** (1 John 1:7). If we are children of light, walking in that light, we have perpetual cleansing from sin. One does not need to be a scholar or theologian to understand that there is no cleansing from sin if there is no consistent walking in the light.

John uses this word again in verse 9: ***If* we confess our sins, he is faithful and just to forgive us our sins, and to cleanse us from all unrighteousness.** Again, there can be no forgiveness and right standing with God, if there is no confession of sins.

I urge you again, do not let anyone influence your thinking on such important doctrines. You can read. Accept what God says in His Word.

The "ifs" are plentiful and always signify conditions. Obey them. When we fail to obey the laws of the land, we pay for it. It is doubly important to keep God's conditions.

He did all He could do for us when He gave us Jesus His Son. Jesus paid it all. He shed His blood and ransomed us. It is only as we are continually found "in Him," being quick to confess our sins and weaknesses, and walking in His light, that we are ready to go "in a moment," without need of time to make things right with God and our fellow man.

3
Carry an Extra Supply

In Chapter 25 of the Gospel of Matthew, our Lord Jesus taught about those who thought they were ready to meet the bridegroom (i.e. the church which was to be in readiness to meet the Lord). All parables taught by Jesus contain many facets of truth.

Some theologians teach that this parable is only for the Jewish nation. However, according to Jewish law, if Jesus was referring only to Jews and not Christians, then the five foolish virgins would have gone back to a priest with an animal sacrifice.

Parables contain truth, without explaining the truth; but we know that church doctrine cannot be based on parables. However, all do agree that they can support doctrine.

What is clear is that our Lord Jesus *would never use a parable to teach a lie.* One religious group teaches that there will be no hell, and declare the story of the rich man and Lazarus to be a parable. We are reminded that, in telling parables, Jesus never mentioned names as He did when He related stories. The account of the rich man and Lazarus is not a parable, but a true story of two men.

The horrible indictment against such false teaching is that this kind of interpretation shows our Lord using a parable to teach an untruth! Jesus is the Truth. He could not use a parable to teach a lie.

Modern-day theologians accept two of the parables in Matthew 25, but reject one as not relating to the Church today. It never ceases to be an amazement how they can accept one parable and reject another in the same chapter.

Can the reason be simply because it does not fit their theology?

Please notice carefully what our Lord Jesus taught which has to apply to all believers of all ages. The desire is to be the bride of the Son of God and be forever with Him. This is true of both the Old Testament church and the New Testament church. All believers have this same desire. According to Adam Clarke, this parable teaches both "the state of the Jews and professing Christians."[1]

If the Bible teaches that once you are called God's child, you can never lose that standing, then at least half of the Bible is wasted time and space. If it is true that you cannot lose your salvation, then this parable of Jesus, along with the parable of the prodigal son, suggests something that is untrue.

Let us look at the parable closely. Jesus called all ten of the principal characters "virgins." Adam Clarke states that "virgins denote the purity of the Christian doctrine and character."[2] Those five who were foolish had hearts that once were illuminated and warmed by their faith, but they had become backslidden from the salvation of God through their carelessness.

Please note that Jesus taught that all of the virgins had their lamps, with oil, and that their lamps were shining. All ten virgins were there with their lamps, equally desiring to see and be with the bridegroom.

Jesus taught that because the bridegroom did not come when they were ready, all ten of them went to sleep. When the call came, only five of them were prepared because they

---

[1]Adam Clarke, *The Holy Bible Containing the Old & New Testaments With Commentary and Critical Notes,* Vol. 3 (Nashville: Abingdon), p. 236.

[2]Clarke, p. 237.

had brought an "extra supply of oil," but there was no hope for the five foolish virgins who were not prepared!

Oil is a type of both the Holy Spirit and the Word of God: **Thy word is a lamp unto my feet, and a light unto my path** (Ps. 119:105). In this parable the Lord taught that there will be those who were at one time ready. . .had His coming been timed to their readiness! Jesus also taught that it is not enough to do "just enough to get by"! We all must carry an extra supply of the Spirit and grace of God. It is always available to the seeking heart.

In this parable Jesus taught that Christians cannot give away to another believer their supply of oil (or the grace or Word they have hidden in their hearts). Each must bear his own burden to be ready for any emergency, especially the Lord's coming! There will be no time to prepare when He comes. One must be ready at all times. This is why it is stated so often, "Be ye ready."

How many professing Christians are watching for and expecting His return? How many are spiritually asleep? How many allow others to dig for their supply of spiritual things so vital to their spiritual survival? How many not only truly believe they are ready and prepared, but are actually looking for Him to come daily? How many? Jesus taught, in this parable, that fifty percent were not ready and would not go in to the bridegroom.

Reader, are you prepared, ready, looking for, and expecting Him? Is your light shining with an extra supply of God's provision of Spirit and grace? I do hope so.

The Lord said to the foolish virgins, through a closed door, "I never knew you." How could He say that? Because God "counts those things that are not as though they were." (See Wycliffe commentary, page 1195.) *At one time they were ready but that was of no value because they were not ready when He came.*

Jesus taught elsewhere that there were two in the field, but only one was taken. There were two grinding at the mill, but only one was taken! Be ready! Be ready to be part of the fifty percent who are carrying the extra supply. Don't do just "enough to get by." Always go the second mile in spiritual matters, just as the Lord Jesus taught us to do.

What is the one outstanding characteristic of the foolish Christian? He not only does just enough to get by, he also carries no extra supply. He depends on others. Christian believer, as we enter these last days, do more, not less. Read the Bible more, pray more, gather with other believers more! (Heb. 10:25.)

4

A "Would-Be" Anti-Christ

Some time ago it was my pleasure to be introduced to a man by the name of Larry Goshorn. I had heard of the remarkable experience of this man and was most anxious to be able to interview him. The following chapter is a summation of what I learned in extended visits with Larry. I am sure you will agree that his story is most unusual and exciting.

My introduction to Larry was an astounding one, inasmuch as he was presented to me as one who "thought he would be the anti-Christ." My curiosity and interest were high when we met, and I found him to be quiet-mannered and unassuming, but with an action-packed life story.

Larry was brought up in a Christian home but was exposed to much evil through an uncle who used to take him to houses of prostitution when he was only five years old. As a result of these experiences and his feelings of being rejected by his mother, he came into a state of rebellion.

While still a young child he saw the movie, "The Devil and Daniel Webster." He saw that selling one's soul to the devil was an act of one's own volition. Because of the rejection in his own life, he felt that happiness and fulfillment would come only from wealth and power in the world. He decided that was what he wanted. He simply said, as Daniel Webster had done in the movie, "Look, Satan, I want to make a contract with you. I want to exchange my soul for the wealth and power of this world."

By the time Larry was in his early thirties, he had arrived at a position of relative power and wealth. He had determined to find the "biggest game in town." His purpose was to get above the law in the world of stocks and bonds. This took place when he was in his early twenties, so by the time he had reached thirty years of age he had become connected with people in the wealth and power group. He knew this was the group who would put the world leader in place. He was a part of this group...and though he knew he was only a pawn and at the bottom end of the scale...still he was in and had a shot at power and fortune. He knew he had connections, worldly wisdom, and talent.

His introduction into the world of computers came when he was in the Navy. He was on board a ship during an air raid drill. During the mock attack he saw sailors being thrown off the gun turrets as they tried to load and reload. When he asked what was causing the problem, he was told that the computers which regulated the guns had gone out of control.

This was in the early fifties, and right then and there he began a quest in his soul, so to speak, to conquer the world! He had a vision of computers controlling machines and being able to make things happen automatically! He started his study of computer technology at age eighteen in the Navy and by the time he was twenty-five he had received his graduate degree in that type of work.

In the sixties he became a Christian and renounced the works of Satan in his life. His mother and father had renewed their walk with the Lord and had begun to earnestly intercede for his salvation. God was faithful to answer their prayers.

Larry was standing outside his home one night and saw a vision. It was like great jagged mountain peaks, with one higher than all the rest. He knew it was symbolic of his life. He saw those peaks and it was as if he had always been headed for one higher than the others...as if he had been heading toward becoming a world leader. The Lord spoke to him and said, "Larry, if you accomplish the climbing of that peak, then what?"

Instantly he knew that the only thing to go for after reaching the summit was immortality. That brought him face to face with decision! After he had conquered all there was to conquer here. . .he would not have attained immortality. In that moment he opened his heart to the Lord. It was as if he had been hit by a lightning bolt and instantly he knew three things: 1) that he would live forever, 2) that the weight of sin was gone, and 3) that he had love in his heart.

By that time of his life he had formed a computer company. In about 1971 the Lord spoke to him and said, "I am going to use this technology for My glory, and I want you to stay with it." Soon after this incident, his company had an opportunity to bid on a contract for a new organization being formed in Brussels called SWIFT: The Society for World Bank of Interchange of Financial Telecommunications. This network would join together all the banks of Europe, and eventually all the banks of the world.

Christians came and asked him if he didn't know that what he was building was the system that would be used for the mark of the beast and for the control of the world. At that time he didn't know anything about the mark of the beast or the book of Revelation. He went to the Lord and said, "God, if this is from Satan, I need to know; I don't want to do it. I want to do Your will."

God spoke immediately and said, "Larry, these are My prophecies and I am bringing them to pass. Even if you won't do these things — the rocks will, in order that these prophecies be fulfilled."

The work was finished in 1977 and there was an inauguration ceremony in the Belgian Palace in Brussels.

During one of our visits, I asked Larry how he thought the anti-Christ would use the European Common Market in his plans. Larry said that there is another system being added. It is far more advanced in Europe than anywhere else in the world. It is a new 3D high-definition technology which will be used in imaging. This will implement the image of the beast technology which has to be in place before the takeover by the anti-Christ. So there are two technologies: one, the mark of the beast system, and the other the image of the beast system. The mark of the beast is well under way, and the image of the beast has been set in motion.

5
"666"

The number 666 is very significant in relation to the computers being used today. Inasmuch as God's Word tells us that we can, with wisdom, figure out the number of the beast in Revelation 13:18, let us do so. If the Bible said that we could not figure this out and understand it, then this effort would be unscriptural and fruitless and a waste of time.

> **Here is wisdom, Let him that hath understanding count the number of the beast: for it is the number of a man; and his number is Six hundred threescore and six.**
>
> **Revelation 13:18**

We could paraphrase this verse and say: "Let him who desires to understand have insight into the man who will kill all who do not take his number. Let this person know that it is easy to know about the worldwide, controlled trading system. You can know what this numbering system is all about for it is a common number among men, the number 666."

The *New King James Version* renders this verse: **Here is wisdom. Let him who has understanding *calculate* the number of the beast, for it is the number of a man: His number is 666.**

In computer terminology the value of each letter advances in increments of six. Thus A is 6; B is 12; C is 18; D is 24; and so on, to the end of the alphabet. If you total the sum of each letter in the word "computer," you will have the number 666.

A worldwide computer system is already in use for trading and identification of criminals. The air waves are flooded with the constant usage of these systems. As knowledge continues to increase at an amazing rate, one can well understand that we are only a few years away from such an advanced computer system that will enable the whole world to be controlled, numbered, and ruled.

Please give special attention to what happens if a person does not cooperate with this worldwide trading system. He cannot buy or sell. If he cannot go to the market place to purchase food, he cannot eat. Millions will be forced to go into this system, for no other reason than just to be able to put food on their table for their children.

Notice also that all who do not take this mark of the beast, either in their foreheads or in their hands, will not only suffer hunger, they will also be killed.

If, on the other hand, an individual does become a worshipper of Satan and takes his mark, then he will suffer the wrath of God that will be poured out. (All this is described in Revelation 14:9-12; 16:2.)

If you read this book after the Church has been taken out of the world, please notice the following verses and receive encouragement:

> **And I saw another sign in heaven, great and marvellous, seven angels having the seven last plagues; for in them is filled up the wrath of God.**
>
> ***And I saw as it were a sea of glass mingled with fire: and them that had gotten the victory over the beast, and over his image, and over his mark, and over the number of his name, stand on the sea of glass, having the harps of God.***
>
> **And they sang the song of Moses the servant of God, and the song of the Lamb, saying, Great and marvellous are thy works, Lord God Almighty; just and true are thy ways, thou King of saints.**
>
> **Who shall not fear thee, O Lord, and glorify thy name? for thou art holy: for all nations shall come and worship before thee; for thy judgments are made manifest.**
>
> **Revelation 15:1-4**

Please note that these people do not experience the wrath of God.

If you, through the strength of the Lord, win the victory over the beast and over his image, over his mark and the number 666. . .you will have won a far greater victory than the empty reward of being accepted by neighbors and having food on your table — though it will mean the laying down of your life.

If you take the number of the beast, you will have only a very few more years to live. No more than seven years. . .and maybe as few as three and a half. Then you will have to face the wrath of God forever. If you refuse to take the number and do not worship Satan, you will be rewarded for your martyrdom forever.

> **And I saw an angel come down from heaven, having the key of the bottomless pit and a great chain in his hand.**
>
> **And he laid hold on the dragon, that old serpent, which is the Devil, and Satan, and bound him a thousand years,**
>
> **And cast him into the bottomless pit, and shut him up, and set a seal upon him, that he should deceive the nations no more, till the thousand years should be fulfilled: and after that he must be loosed a little season.**
>
> **And I saw thrones, and they sat upon them, and judgment was given unto them: and I saw the souls of them that were beheaded, for the *witness of Jesus, and of the word of God,* and which had *not* worshipped the beast, neither his image, neither had received his mark upon their foreheads, or in their hands; and they lived and reigned with Christ a thousand years.**
>
> **But the rest of the dead lived not again until the thousand years were finished. This is the first resurrection.**
>
> **Revelation 20:1-5**

What a glorious reward you will receive forever! To be with an eternal, loving Father and saints of all ages, as well as with your own loved ones. Those who enter heaven through martyrdom are also rewarded by reigning with Christ on earth for a period of a thousand years.

Please notice that in the first through the fifth verse of Revelation 20, two groups of people are described. First, those who are martyred for their witness of Jesus (Gentiles) and those who are killed because they have faith in God's Word.

I believe that the second group will be those Jews who believe in the Old Testament and God's commandments. (Rev. 14:12.) They know they are to worship God and God alone...no one else. I personally believe that there are millions of Jews who will be killed by the anti-Christ. They will not bow down to him, nor worship him. It seems that God has always honored, from the very beginning, those who will die rather than bow the knee to any god but Him.

Hitler, along with other rulers down through the ages, discovered that the Jews will not bow down, nor give their allegiance to any god other than the God of Abraham.

6
The Anti-Christ System

The emergence of a second anti-Christ in Revelation 13 has been little noted by Bible scholars. In verse 11, the writer beheld another beast *coming up out of the earth*. This seems amazing! Shouldn't the first one be sufficient to do Satan's work? It seems to be reasonable that the first anti-Christ was a person, and though he was filled with and controlled by Satan, he was but a man.

As such, after experiencing assassination and resurrection, he could have great fear and apprehension that another attempt could be made on his life. So now we see the plan.

Please note in Revelation 13:1 that the first anti-Christ is seen "rising up out of the sea." This is a person. The second anti-Christ, in verse 11, comes up "out of the earth," and is not a human being. He is made of that which is in the earth. This second anti-Christ is comprised of materials such as minerals and ore, products that come from the earth. He is similar to a robot, one which has been given the power to speak and the ability to rule.

He will be fully empowered by Satan and will cause all people to continue to worship the first beast whose deadly wound was healed. This second beast will speak as Satan speaks. He will have great miracle-working power. Whereas the first beast did not seem to be able to succeed in getting all of the people on earth to worship him and Satan, this second beast will convince them by threat of death.

Many who yet have faith in God, whether Jew or Gentile, will be deceived by this great entity. He will have unlimited power, given to him by Satan, to do great miracles. Verses 13 and 14 speak of his awesome power, even the authority to call down fire from above.

By this time, dear reader, if you are still on earth, you will have to exercise the greatest faith possible in order to believe and cling to the Word of God. You must not be swayed in your belief, no matter how great and fearful are the miracles performed by this second anti-Christ.

Notice that this second anti-Christ will cause an *image* to be made to the first beast. Satan will cause it to live, and it is he who will begin to kill those who refuse to worship before it.

Now you must pay very special attention to this segment describing the anti-Christ. The satanic assault on your soul and mind which you will have experienced up to now, will seem as nothing in the light of what will soon come to pass. Now you will begin to see wholesale slaughter and martyrdom on every hand. There will emerge a new form of government totally controlled by Satan.

The devil, from the very beginning of his existence, has desired to sit as God on a throne and have the whole world bow in worship to him. Indicative of this great desire is the fact that his very first effort to tempt our Lord was to persuade Him to bow down before him. (Matt. 4:8-10.)

He will now begin to fulfill this hunger for worship by killing everyone on earth who will not bow to him. He will bring his plan to pass by implementing a system of total dominance. He will control where people work, what they buy and sell, when and where they travel; everyone will be totally subservient to his will. According to Revelation 13:15, Satan will accomplish all this through the image of the beast.

The whole earth will be forced to have a number, much like our Social Security number, only it will begin with the number 666 and perhaps end with it.

The name of the beast will become the trademark for all the market places in the world. All commerce, worldwide, will be controlled by Satan and the numbering system.

This system of numbering will involve the billions of people living on earth. It will take an enormous computer system to control it. This is the only way that Satan can force his will on all mankind. Everyone will have to work in order to exist. Because everyone must buy and sell and eat, no one will be able to escape detection.

Pay no attention to the books you may have read about escaping to the mountains, caves, and dens with dehydrated food! This will not be possible inasmuch as the Bible clearly states that all who do not worship the beast will be killed. (v. 15.) The Bible nowhere gives hope for survival, with the exception of the 144,000 Jews who somehow escape.

Many believe that the seat of this awesome power system will come from the European Common Market. In 1992 ten, and up to twelve, nations will form one great United States of Europe. The headquarters, at this present writing, is in Brussels, Belgium.

There is an enormous computer system already in place in Brussels and it is called "the beast." I have seen the code that taps into this computerized trading system. It is 666-666-666-666-. Many people believe that by 1992 this market will become so powerful that the whole earth will be forced to trade with it.

Dear reader, please do not capitulate. Do not give in and comply with this system. Please read, and reread, the chapter instructing you about the things you can do to receive the necessary strength and help from Almighty God. You can yet make heaven your eternal home. It is not too late.

7
The Question of the Rapture

There are many who write against the rapture. There are those who preach and teach against such an event. Some teach that we will go half-way (or three and a half years) into the reign of the anti-Christ before this great event takes place. There are others who teach that we will go all the way through the reign of the anti-Christ to the literal second coming of Christ — thus there will be no rapture. Some even teach that there will be no rapture, no millennium, and no second advent of Christ. All read the same Bible, all are intelligent, and all believe they are right!

The tremendous danger in the espousing of all these various positions is that many of God's precious saints are confused. They are not only confused, but are not preparing for our Lord Jesus to come suddenly "as a thief in the night." Again, not only are they confused, they are also not living the dedicated, separated, consecrated lifestyle that they would be following if they truly expect His coming at any moment.

Jesus gives us warning in Matthew 24:44 (and also in Luke 12:40): **Therefore be ye also ready: for in such an hour as ye think not the Son of man cometh.** The *Twentieth Century New Testament version of this verse reads,* **. . . it is just when you are least expecting him that the Son of Man will come.**

> **And while they went to buy, the bridegroom came; and they that were *ready* went in with him to the marriage: and the door was shut.**
>
> **Matthew 25:10**

> **Let us be glad and rejoice, and give honour to him: for the marriage of the Lamb is come, and his wife *hath made herself ready.***
>
> **Revelation 19:7**

In the Greek, the word translated "ready" is a command in the continuous action.

Teachings that do not emphasize Christ's immediate return will also fail to emphasize the daily looking for, and expectancy, of His appearance:

> **Looking** (Greek present participle, continuous action) **for that blessed hope, and the glorious appearing of the great God and our Saviour Jesus Christ.**
>
> **Titus 2:13**

> **. . .and unto them that look for him shall he appear the second time without sin unto salvation.**
>
> **Hebrews 9:28**

The Amplified Bible version of this verse reads: **. . .but to bring to full salvation those who are (eagerly, constantly and patiently) waiting for and expecting Him.**

> **Watch** (imperative tense, a command to do something in the future which requires continuous action) **therefore — give strict attention, be cautious and active — for you do not know in what kind of a day [whether a near or remote one] your Lord is coming.**
>
> **Matthew 24:42 AMP**

Certainly one cannot be ready for something he is not expecting. There was a humorous song a few years ago, "If I'da knew you was comin', I'da baked a cake!" Readiness and expectancy go hand in hand.

Our Lord Jesus warned the church of the Laodiceans that they would be spewed out of His mouth because they were neither cold nor hot, thus not ready. (Rev. 3:15,16.)

Even if this author is wrong and there is no rapture, I had rather err in warning the Church to be ready for the sudden return of Christ (or of untimely death), than to be indifferent to the volume of scriptural evidence that shows forth this important event. To do so would place me in danger of being responsible for the careless living of saints which will, for them, cancel out their hope of heaven.

Again let me say, this book is not written to prove other positions wrong. It is written to warn Christians to be ready. Each of us is only one heartbeat away from facing eternal judgment. To be constantly ready, watching for and expecting Christ's return, just seems to be good spiritual reasoning.

8
Overcoming Saints

Be not unequally yoked together with unbelievers: for what fellowship hath righteousness with unrighteousness? and what communion hath light with darkness?

2 Corinthians 6:14

Having therefore these promises, dearly beloved, let us cleanse ourselves from all filthiness of the flesh and spirit, perfecting holiness in the fear of God.

2 Corinthians 7:1

Follow peace with all men, and holiness, without which no man shall see the Lord:

Looking diligently lest any man fail of the grace of God....

Hebrews 12:14,15

Wuest interprets 1 John 3:3 in this way: **And everyone who has this hope continually set on Him is constantly purifying himself just as that One is pure.**

A *true believer* is one who has received Jesus Christ and has made Him Lord of all. This believer is cleansed by the blood of God's Son. His name is written in the Book of Life. Yet he must not allow Satan or the world to pull him away. We are warned to resist Satan and to take on all the armor of God to do battle against him. (James 4:7; 1 Pet. 5:9; Eph. 6:11-17.)

Here, in this text, we are warned against being unequally yoked together with unbelievers and fellowshipping with them. We are to come from among them, to be separate, and not to touch the unclean thing. This warning includes far more than courtship and marriage.

It there is never any danger in losing one's salvation, then Paul's warnings are out of God's will and Paul did not write through the inspiration of God's Spirit.

Paul did speak by the Holy Spirit, and he taught that it is possible for a believer to become yoked together with unbelievers again. In his commentary, Adam Clarke states that this word *yoke* is a military term meaning to "keep in your own ranks." It is impossible for righteousness to fellowship with unrighteousness. Paul, knowing the Corinthians, must have been aware of this yoking, or bonding with the heathen in fellowship. Any time a Christian continues in doing the opposite of God's will, he destroys all that God has done for him, or will ever be able to do, if he does not change. Paul's warnings are combined with his questions.

We must ask ourselves these same questions. They will apply to the last part of this age even more than to Paul's day because there will be no time for Christians to repent when Jesus comes as a thief in the night, without warning. (1 Thess. 5:2; 1 Pet. 3:10.)

The instruction to refuse to be yoked with sinners is followed by the question, "How can righteousness fellowship (be intimate) with unrighteousness?" Can a Christian, day after day, fellowship with people who reject Christianity and have only thought for this life? The Apostle Paul says that it is impossible.

Can light mix with darkness in close, intimate communion? The Greek word translated "communion" is *koinonia*. It is an intimate term and refers only to fellowship between those who live in the light.

Can Christ and the devil harmonize?

Can the temple of God agree with the temple of Satan?

Can a believer be in concord with an atheist?

The answer to all of these questions is an emphatic NO!

Since we, as believers, are the temple of God, then the above is not only incompatible, but totally *impossible.* Can the temple of God (which you and I are) attend Hollywood productions that are the temple of Satan, masquerading as harmless entertainment? The great majority of movies and television programs issuing forth today are filled with sex, violence, rape, murder, and all kinds of mayhem. Prisoners, arrested for committing violent acts, have confessed to having been influenced by something they saw on film. If you are a parent, I beg of you to be aware of what your children are watching! You influence them greatly by your own example.

I tremble for the Christian whose lifestyle dictates attendance at the latest film out. . . regardless of its content! Is it possible to become "yoked together" (addicted) and not be aware of it?

Paul finishes with one last plea to the Christians at Corinth, thus to the Christians now alive: "Come out from among them and be separate." To those who will not commune with or have fellowship with the ungodly, the Lord promises that they will be received and that He will be a Father to them and they will become His sons and daughters.

The last verse of 1 Corinthians 6 should be the first verse of Chapter 7. In essence, it reads, "Let us cleanse ourselves from all the things that pollute the flesh and thus creep over into the spirit realm." Adam Clarke's commentary puts it so well, "But if we do not withhold the food by which the man of sin is nourished and supported, we cannot expect God to purify our hearts."[1]

---

[1]Adam Clarke, *The Holy Bible Containing the Old & New Testaments With Commentary and Critical Notes*, VOL. 3 (Nashville: Abingdon), p. 344.

The injunction to come out, to be separate, is in the aorist tense, the imperative. It is a command, something that must be obeyed. "Let us cleanse ourselves" is in the same Greek mode; it is final, it must be done.

A heart for holiness is a heart for God. Holiness is a state of continual sanctification.

If we cannot cleanse ourselves, then the Apostle Paul has commanded us to do the impossible. But it is possible. If we fail to take heed to God's warning, we cannot remain in Christ our Lord and He is not Lord over all.

One's will is not surrendered at conversion. It remains an integral part of God's original plan for mankind. A person can change his mind, become careless about his experience, backslide, apostasize, and lose out on eternity.

Do not let the experience of others interpret this great subject for you. Do your own searching of the Scriptures, paying special attention to the writings of the Apostle Paul and John, the Beloved Disciple.

The warning to Christians in 1 John 2:15 reads: **Love not the world, neither the things that are in the world. If any man love the world, the love of the Father is not in him.**

The word translated "world" (Gr: *kosmos*) refers to the organized working of Satan who is termed the prince, leader, and god of this age. A Christian must follow a highly organized spiritual lifestyle, inasmuch as the world system is organized with the specific purpose of pulling him away from God — even as that same evil system pulled the prodigal son away from the father's house. (Luke 15.)

The prodigal son's father said of him after he had returned, **...my son was *dead*, and is alive again; he was *lost*, and is found...**(Luke 15:24). Note that the son was born of his father and lived as a son in his house. Jesus taught that he was saved. The organized system of that day lured him away into a riotous, wasteful lifestyle.

In this parable Jesus indicated that the young man was a son but left of his own free will, and became dead to his father, and was lost. The father did not send for the son, nor did he go searching for him. The lost son looked at his plight, changed his mind (his will) and came back from his deplorable lifestyle. He was immediately welcomed and reinstated as his father's beloved son. It is possible to receive Jesus as Savior and be gloriously saved; but, with time, that glorious experience can erode away until the person no longer resists the pull of this present world, and thus becomes lost.

Christian, be ready, for the Lord is coming "in such an hour as ye think not." (Matt. 24:44.) He will not time His coming to coincide with your readiness. You must time your readiness for His coming. Be alert to the age in which we are now living. Live in a constant state of self-cleansing and self-purifying. Satan desires to have you. He is not after the sinner; he already has him. He is after you. Do not let happen to you what has happened to so many others who were just as committed, or even more committed, than you. Will to feed and nourish your inner man with the Word of God and be strong in the Lord. Do not allow a spirit of lukewarmness, bitterness, worldliness, or any other deceiving spirit to become a part of your lifestyle!

Remember, salvation is only secure — in Christ.

9

In My Father's House

In My Father's house there are many dwelling places (homes). If it were not so, I would have told you, for I am going away to prepare a place for you.

And when (if) I go and make ready a place for you, I will come back again and will take you to Myself, that where I am you may be also.

John 14:2,3 AMP

Beck's translation of this verse reads, **. . . I'll come again and take you home with Me. . . .**

Assured that He Who raised up the Lord Jesus will raise us up also with Jesus and bring us [along] with you into His presence.

2 Corinthians 4:14 AMP

The neo-theology that mocks the rapture teaching has attracted the interest of some writers in the New Age movement. They are delighted that this new post-tribulation teaching (no rapture. . .just Christ returning to the earth) does away with that which is literal by spiritualizing it away.

This new teaching, which is gaining a large group of followers, leaves the true Church on earth to face not only the wrath of Satan, but also (if there is no rapture and they remain on earth) the wrath of an angry God.

This new concept, which has been formulated, teaching that Christ will not "snatch" the believers away but will leave us here, does not allow for the fulfillment of Revelation 16 when the wrath of God is poured out upon the earth. This spiritualizing away of the rapture of the true Church does not pencil out in sound reasoning. It has God pictured as pouring out His wrath and anger on His own Church for whom His Son gave His life to redeem.

Those who would spiritualize away our Christian hope of being caught away have of necessity also spiritualized away our text for this chapter. They would have us believe that our Lord Jesus did not really mean what He said. He is not really preparing for us a physical place (a mansion) so we can be in heaven in His Father's house with Him. No. They speak of that which we believe to be literal as just being fancies, or vacuums, or "spiritual" abodes (houses) on earth and not with the Father in heaven as Jesus taught.

If they can spiritualize away this truth, then they might as well spiritualize away John 3:16 or John 3:3, which would mean that we are not really born again of the Spirit. This could be carried even further to spiritualize away hell! These are preposterous thoughts!

Once theologians begin to do away with literal truth, there is no assessing how far they will go. This explaining away of sacred literal truth led to the demise of the Church in the third and fourth centuries. Are we heading in that direction again?

These same theologians not only do away with the rapture, but also with the literal reign of Christ on earth during the millennium. The early Church fathers taught, for three hundred years, a literal millennial rule of our Lord Jesus. This was taught up to the time of the Council of Nicea (A.D. 325). The book of Revelation refers to the millennium many times.

In times past this same manner of spiritualizing has led to an anti-Semitic spirit. This spirit says that God owes the Jews nothing. This theology gives no place to the dispensations as we have known them. Did God deal at one time exclusively with the Jews in the animal sacrifices for sin? Yes. Is there not now a dispensation of grace and the Church Age? Yes. Will He again reinstate Israel to full fellowship as He, in so many places, has promised? Yes. Think what an enrichment and greater advantage will follow their full reinstatement. (Rom. 1:12 AMP.)

If John 14:2,3 does not promise the believer a literal, physical place to be forever with the Lord, it does not teach anything! Jesus said, "If it were not so, I would have told you."

Notice the rapture teaching in John 14:3 which parallels the Apostle Paul's teaching to the churches: **...I will come again...** For what? **...and receive you** (the literal Greek is "take you") **unto myself....**

This is not what Jesus taught in Matthew 24. There He taught that all tribes and all peoples will see Him come back to earth. Jesus taught Paul personally about taking the believers to be with Him, and here He is teaching the disciples the same. When everyone sees Him return to earth (Matt. 24), we will be with Him!

I invite you to enjoy the rendering of this promise in John 14:3 by various scholars:

...I shall come back to take you with me....(ABUV)

...I shall return and take you to be with me....(TCNT)

...I'll come again and take you home with Me....(BECK)

...I am coming back; and then I will take you to myself....(KNOX)

Dear reader, do not allow anyone to spiritualize away your hope. Jesus did not lie to us. He explained in a few words the difference between the rapture (the saints going home) and His second coming (when He returns to the earth to rule and reign).

Second Corinthians 4:14 has been overlooked as a rapture promise, but it is one. Paul is referring to his going ahead of the Church in death. But do not let that be a problem. He seems to be saying: "For Jesus will raise me up." (He is speaking of resurrection from the dead.) Paul so strongly believed the rapture would take place soon after his death that he placed the Corinthians in the rapture by saying, "...and (He) will bring us (me) to His presence with you." I have paraphrased this, so please read it for yourself. *The Amplified Bible* states it very clearly.

Notice, "...bring us into His presence." Jesus is not going to come back to earth and join us here. We, along with Paul and all other saints, both dead and alive, are going to be taken to be in His presence, in His Father's house (dwelling place, eternal city), to be forever with our Lord in our own separate mansions (abodes, homes). We, as His Church, His Bride, will go where He goes, stay where He stays, rule where He rules — forever, never to be separated.

We have been promised by our Lord and Savior Jesus Christ, Who is the Truth, that He has gone to prepare us a place, and He is going to take us to that place.

Reader, I warn you not to be misled. Your pastor may be a good and godly man. You may have been saved under his ministry and your children dedicated and baptized under his ministry. He may be a good shepherd. But remember, all good shepherds do not necessarily make good theologians. If they teach that there is not going to be a rapture, then, in my opinion, they have been misled. They stand in great danger of taking away from, or adding to, the teaching of God's Word. They, themselves, could not only be out of the will of God, but also leading others astray.

Do not allow anyone, simply because you love and respect him, to deprive you of simple truth, clearly taught. There will be a taking out of this world of the dead saints (the resurrection) and the living saints (the rapture). Believe it, expect it, and be looking for the King of kings and Lord of lords!

Remember, He is coming to take away those "in Christ." Saints who have made Jesus the Lord of their lives. Not merely believers, but active Christians whose lamps are full of oil and burning brightly. Examine your relationship with Him. Are you ready?

10

The Terrible Day of the Anti-Christ

The prophet Ezekiel, looking ahead, well prophesied of the anti-Christ when he said, **. . .Thus saith the Lord God; Because thine heart is lifted up, and thou hast said, I am a God, I sit in the seat of God, in the midst of the *seas*; yet thou art a man, and *not* God, though thou set thine heart as the heart of God** (Ezek. 28:2).

The prophet Daniel also prophesied of his appearance: **And he shall speak great words against the most High, and *shall wear out the saints of the most High*. . .** (Dan. 7:25).

The Apostle Paul clearly and distinctly reveals more in his prophecies in 2 Thessalonians 2. He calls him a man of sin (lawlessness), the son of perdition, an imposter, and a master of iniquity and deceit.

Revelation, Chapter 13, is totally given over to a vivid description of the anti-Christ. If it is possible, please read this entire chapter now. If you, who are reading this book, are in danger of missing the "catching away of the believers," spoken of as "the rapture of the saints," I strongly urge you to read this vital chapter prayerfully and carefully.

You will notice that the one referred to as "the beast" in Revelation 13:1 (hereafter referred to as the anti-Christ) is a man. Just as Daniel prophesied that he would be a person who would attempt to make himself God. Reader, please note carefully that this anti-Christ receives all of his power (authority) from the dragon, who is Satan.

One of the events that will identify him as the anti-Christ is his assassination. This is found in Revelation 13:3. This assassination will be broadcast around the world because he will be a world leader. The first true revelation of whom you will be dealing with will be exposed when his deadly (mortal) wound is healed. This is described in the same verse in Revelation.

This marvelous supernatural miracle will be proclaimed around the world by the news media. Satan worshippers will, overnight, become the leading religious body, and deceive all other religious groups.

Please remember that this person, called the beast in Revelation 13, will represent himself as a very good, capable leader. He will not, until he has gained popularity, allow himself to be identified with the Satanist movement. Revelation 13:4 teaches that, at this time, almost the entire world will worship the dragon (Satan) who raised this man from the dead. Thus, almost all will be forced to accept him.

This great miracle will now cause the anti-Christ to become more militant, blasphemous, and warlike. We understand this because the Bible says in Revelation 13:4, **. . .who is able to make war with him?**

Those who are left on the earth will, at this point, be able to recognize this person by name and will more fully understand the power behind him. No freedom of air time or newspaper publicity will be given to anyone who opposes him. Certainly no religious group or Bible-believing Jews will be recognized.

It is at this time that this anti-Christ (the beast) will openly begin to blaspheme God, Jesus Christ, and the saints who have been raptured (Rev. 13:6) and who now dwell in heaven. At first, and for three and a half years into the tribulation, there will be great peace and prosperity. (Read Dan. 8:23-25.)

In Revelation 13:7 there is evidence that the anti-Christ will make war with the saints. "Saints" here refers to the Jewish people. This same verse reveals that the anti-Christ now has authority over the world, meaning that he has command of the armies, navies, and air forces of the nations.

Dear reader, if the rapture of the saints has already taken place by the time you read this, and you find yourself left behind, I entreat you to carefully study verse eight of the thirteenth chapter of Revelation.

It is probable that you will begin to experience a great deal of discouragement and depression. Thoughts will fill your mind (aided and abetted by Satan) that if your name was written in the Book of Life, you would have gone with your loved ones.

This is exactly what so many millions of believers, because the pull of the world caused them to leave their first love and they missed out, will begin to believe. They will think that all hope is gone, that there is no more chance for them.

Please do not allow yourself to begin to think these thoughts. Do not believe Satan's lie. You do not have to worship him and, by refusing him, you can still have hope.

Your name is written in that book of God, Who by His foreknowledge, looked ahead and saw you refusing to join those who worship Satan. God could see, deep in your heart, the true faith that was there. . . so muted by the lure of temporal worldliness that caused you to miss the rapture. . . but now shining forth as you set yourself to be a man or woman of God. There is now only one way whereby you will be able to spend eternity with your loved ones and with Jesus. It is the same path that so many of God's people down through the ages have trod. . . the path of martyrdom. Though it is a knowledge that everything within you will resist because of the fearfulness of the thought, you must now contemplate it. Just as God gave them grace to die, so He will give it to you.

11
Special Instructions for Those Who Miss the Rapture

The saints who are ready, prepared, and looking for the return of their Lord, as the Apostle Paul taught the young church in 1 Thessalonians 4, will go to be with Him, "and so shall they ever be." But consider the shock and horror of those who have allowed themselves to be deluded into thinking they were ready for the return of the Lord but, instead, discover that they have been lulled into a state of spiritual neglect and thus have missed the rapture.

If the reader of this book is one of these most unfortunate people, you are now destined to fight a fight of faith that very few saints have ever had to wage in two thousand years. You will be forced to do battle with Satan, through a system masterminded by a man totally possessed by the devil, and hosts of unbelievers and scoffers.

This battle will differ from anything you have ever known in that you will not have access to any group or any person for help. You will be able to trust no one. The dictatorship of the one ruling will be complete and absolute. There will be total control over the minds of men, over their families, commerce, and even their leisure time.

Remember, it is Satan who is ruling! He is full of beauty and wisdom. He is cunning personified, and is next only to God in power.

Where God is just. . .he is unjust.

Where God is truth. . .he is a lie.

Where God is righteous. . .he is unrighteous.

Where God is love...he is hate.

Where God forgives...he condemns.

For centuries there have been martyrs who have died for their faith in Jesus. Usually they died at the hand of an opposing fanatical religious group. Afterward, with families and loved ones gathered around who had witnessed the death, fervent prayer was offered up and there was a great strengthening of Christian faith.

For one who is left, after the rapture has taken place, it will be a totally different picture. You will be alone. There will be no one to pray with you and support you. No one will even witness your execution, nor will there be any mention of your name in the news.

Satan, coming to full power through the beast of Revelation 13, immediately will separate and isolate all Christians as they are systematically betrayed and destroyed.

One of the first enemies you will have to contend with in your fight of faith for eternal life is deep resentment against God. **Guard diligently against this damaging emotion. Instead, accept the responsibility for your plight. Confess that it was neglect of your relationship with God that has brought you to this unhappy state.** You need God's help as never before.

Upon realizing that true worshippers have gone and that you must now face the beast who sits in the place of God, who pretends to be God, and who commands worship, **immediately you must determine to get on your knees and repent, repent, repent, before the Lord.**

Many teach that the Holy Spirit will no longer be present as He has been to convict of sin, teach through the Word, and make the presence of God real to believers. However, before (in the Old Testament) and after the day of Pentecost, God has always heard and honored prayer in every age. **Pray and repent, and He will hear you.** His ear has always been open to prayer, and He cannot change.

Please allow me to suggest a prayer. You could pray this prayer:

> "Father God, in the name of Jesus Christ of Nazareth, I come to You. I humble myself in repentence and ask You, in His name, to forgive me of all my sins."
>
> (Hold nothing back; confess all of your sins to Him.)
>
> "I ask You, and will continue to ask You daily, to give me the moral fiber and courage I need to live in refusal to take the mark of the beast. Amen."

You must now stand in the strength of fervent prayer! Whatever you do, you must not take the mark of the beast, for all who do so must face the wrath of God! (Rev. 14:9-11.)

I counsel you to find a Bible. This may be very difficult because all religious literature of any kind will have been confiscated and it will be against the law to have any in your home. It will be extremely difficult to find even one piece of literature about the Bible. This will be hard to believe since we have had such a great quantity of literature available all of our lives. All Christian bookstores will be closed. No Bibles or religious literature of any kind will be found in libraries. There will be no Christian programs on TV or radio, no Christian hotlines to call for prayer, no neighbors who can be trusted...including your own relatives. Your Bible will become your most precious possession.

Begin to read the Bible daily, especially the New Testament. Read particularly the Gospel of John and the epistle of 1 John. Keep in mind that God has always honored His Word in every age. Strength will flow from God into your inner being. Try to memorize certain passages that will minister to you as you meditate upon them through the days and nights. Try to find gospel music and message tapes. They will be difficult to find, and, if you do find them, you must be very secretive about listening to them. If they are discovered, they will be confiscated.

You will be able to trust no one! **Do not take anyone into your confidence.** At this point there will be rewards offered for anyone who betrays a Christian. Remember, Satan himself is in full power and he hates anyone who worships God. The saints who now dwell in heaven are out of his reach.

As you pray and read the Bible daily, you will find peace, and strength will grow within you. As you realize how difficult it is going to be to continue living as a Christian in a police state, you may come to the place where you will reckon it preferable to confess openly that you are a believer and set yourself to accept what this confession will bring.

> "Dear Lord Jesus, Head of Your Church, please help this reader now seeking to have courage to follow Your instructions in this chapter.
>
> "Help this one to repent and read, devour, Your Word...and to believe that You do hear prayer.
>
> "Give strength to live, and, if necessary, to die for believing in You and in Your Word.
>
> "Thank You for hearing this prayer. Amen."

Conclusion

It was a startling thing when the Lord Jesus began to speak to me concerning writing a new book about the Christians who will be left behind when Christ comes for His Bride. It is a subject that is seldom addressed and, when one considers the consequences of not being ready, it is one that should be talked about and squarely faced. I had never before done an in-depth study of this subject.

Revelation 20:4 makes many things clear. It deals directly with the Christians who will be slain by the anti-Christ for refusing to take the mark of the beast (the number 666) on their forehead or on their hands.

The saints who come out of the great tribulation in Revelation 7:13 are different from the ones in Chapter 20. Their reward is very different also. The martyrs in Chapter 7 serve the Lord day and night in His temple. Those who miss the rapture, but refuse to take the mark of the beast and therefore are martyred, have a limited reward. They will reign with Christ for a thousand years only, and then will dwell in the heavenly paradise which lies just outside the eternal foursquare city. This author also believes that this is where the babies and children who die innocently will also live. Both groups will have access to come and go into that great city and worship God.

This manuscript was, for the most part, finished before November of 1989. At that time in history, God began to fulfill the prophecy in Ezekiel 38:4 (NKJ), **"I will turn you around, put hooks into your jaws, and lead you...."** God sovereignly began to prepare all things for the great battle of Armageddon.

In one day the wall of resistance to freedom and the gospel came down. East Germans, many of them for the first time in their life, tasted of freedom and heard the gospel.

Historians and the media are amazed at the sudden, sweeping changes in Russia and the rejection of Communism in favor of new openness by many in the ruling party of Eastern Europe. This begins the fulfillment of Romans 9:28 which speaks of a short, quick work.

The European Common Market nations have already agreed to become the United States of Europe and will come together in 1992. Daniel's vision for the last days of the "ten-toed kingdom" is here. Though, at this writing, there are twelve (and possibly other) nations who will join, only ten will rule because three will be put out. (Read Dan. 7:20,24.)

The author has seen the code card for their computer system. It is a series of sixes, which puts all things into perspective. No one in past history, *in one generation,* has seen the return of Israel to her homeland AND the formation of the ten-toed kingdom.

Surely Christ will return soon! I remember the prophetic words of the Lord Jesus to Kenneth Hagin some years ago, "Before the worst is to come, I will take My people home."

Be ready. The Lord is doing "a short, quick work." Be quick to hear His voice and quick to obey Him. Remember, saints: "There is no sin that can give you enough pleasure worth the penalty."

References

Adam Clarke. *The Holy Bible Containing the Old & New Testaments With a Commentary and Critical Notes,* Vol. 3. Abingdon Press, Nashville, Tennessee.

The Amplified Bible, New Testment (AMP). Copyright © 1958, 1987, by The Lockman Foundation, La Habra, California.

The Holy Bible, New King James Version (NKJ). Copyright© 1982 by Thomas Nelson, Inc., Nashville, Tennessee.

The New Testament: An Expanded Translation by Kenneth S. Wuest. Copyright© 1961 by Wm. B. Eeardmans Publishing Co., Grand Rapids, Michigan.

The New Testament in the Language of Today (BECK) by William F. Beck. Copyright© 1963 by Concordia Publishing House, St. Louis, Missouri.

The New Testament in Modern English, Rev. Ed. Copyright© 1958, 1960, 1972 by J.B. Phillips. Published by the Macmillan Publishing Co., Inc., New York, New York.

The New Testament in the Translation of Monsignor Ronald Knox (KNOX) © 1944 by Sheed and Ward, Inc., New York, with the kind permission of his Eminence the Cardinal Archbishop of Westminster and Burns and Oates, Ltd.

The New Testament of Our Lord and Savior (ABUV) by John A. Broadus© United Bible Society. American Bible Union Version (Improved Edition).

The Twentieth Century New Testament (TNCT). Published by Moody Bible Institute.

Books by Roy H. Hicks

Obtaining Bible Promises
A Different Approach for Every Promise

Keys of the Kingdom

Instrument Rated Christian

Healing Your Insecurities

Praying Beyond God's Ability
Why Prayers Go Unanswered

Use It Or Lose It
The Word of Faith

He Who Laughs Lasts...And Lasts...And Lasts

Another Look At The Rapture

The Power of Positive Resistance
The Christian's Antihistamine

Whatever Happened to Hope?

Another Look at Angels

Bodily Healing and The Atonement
(Dr. T. J. McCrossan)

Final Days...and Counting
Containing Instructions for Those
Who Miss His Coming

Books by Margaret Hicks

A Christian Woman's Answer to Aging